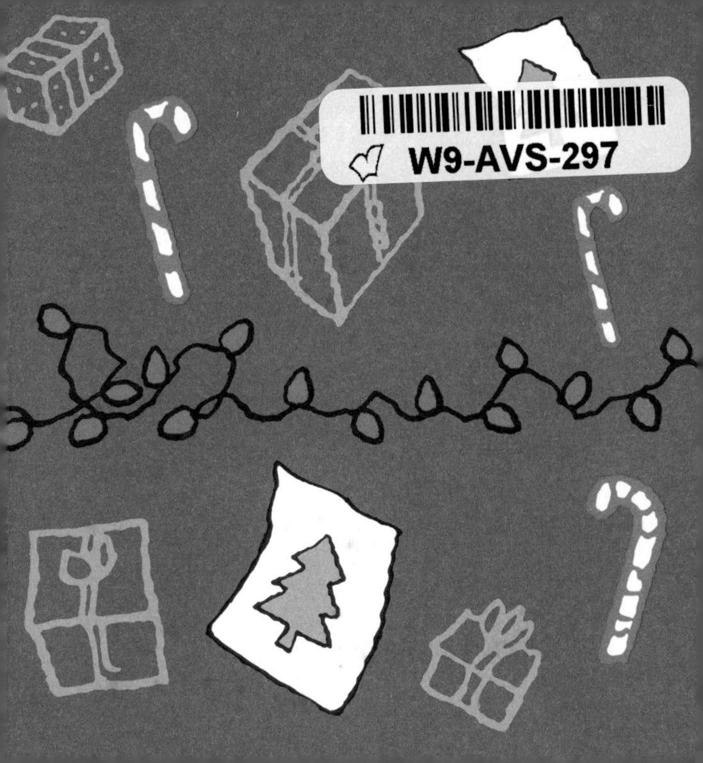

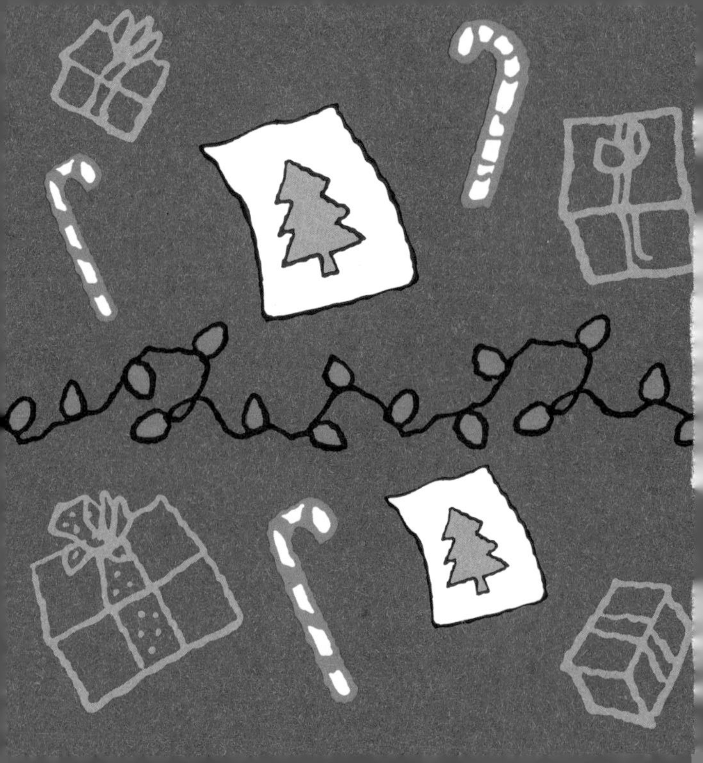

Lighten Up, It's Christmas!

by

SCHULZ

HarperHorizon

An Imprint of HarperCollins*Publishers*

Dear Mr. Claus

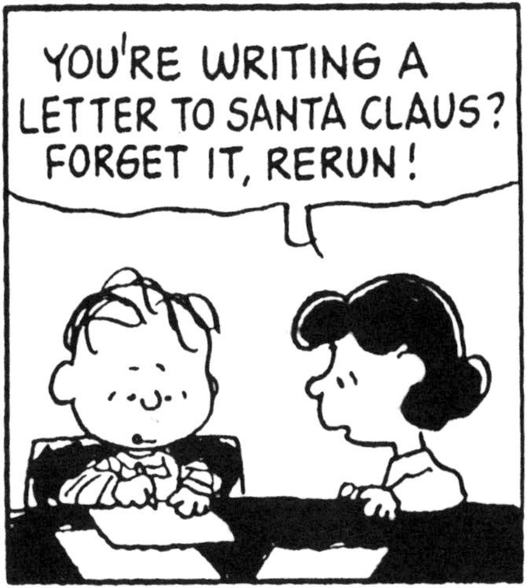
YOU'RE WRITING A LETTER TO SANTA CLAUS? FORGET IT, RERUN!

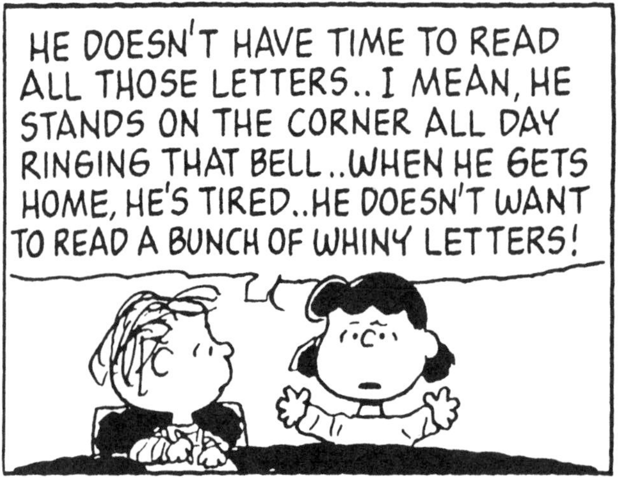
HE DOESN'T HAVE TIME TO READ ALL THOSE LETTERS.. I MEAN, HE STANDS ON THE CORNER ALL DAY RINGING THAT BELL..WHEN HE GETS HOME, HE'S TIRED..HE DOESN'T WANT TO READ A BUNCH OF WHINY LETTERS!

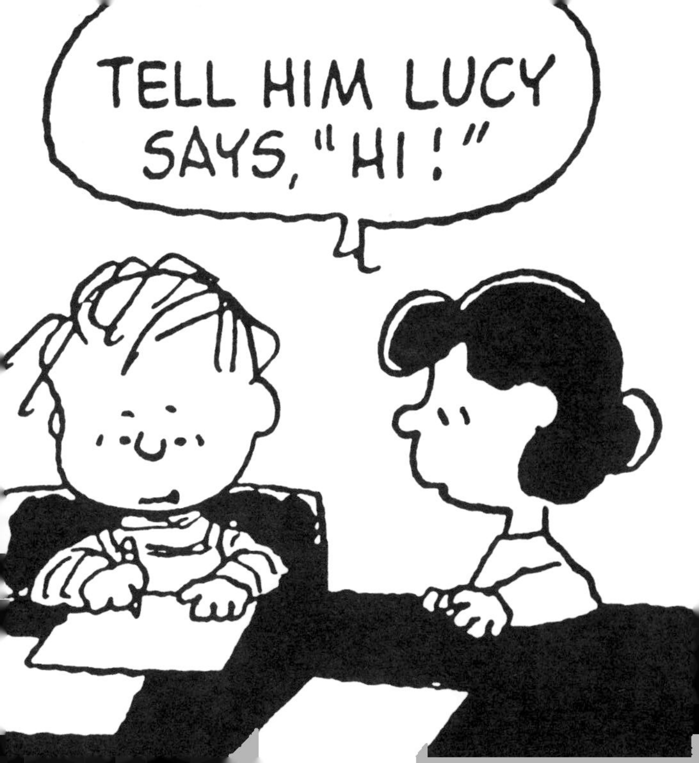
TELL HIM LUCY SAYS, "HI!"

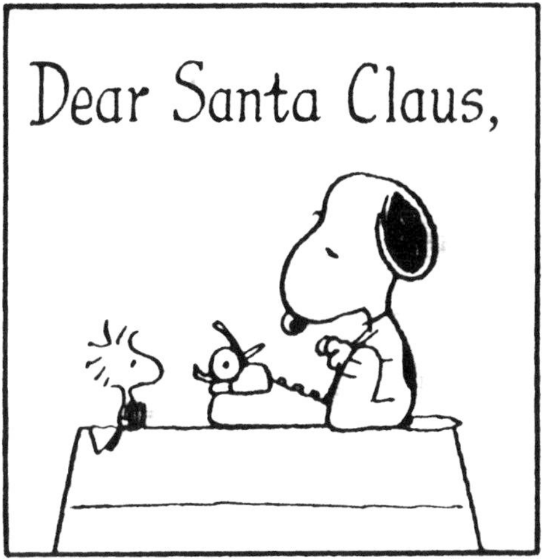
Dear Santa Claus,

OKAY, NOW YOU TELL ME WHAT YOU WANT HIM TO BRING YOU, AND I'LL PUT IT IN THE LETTER...

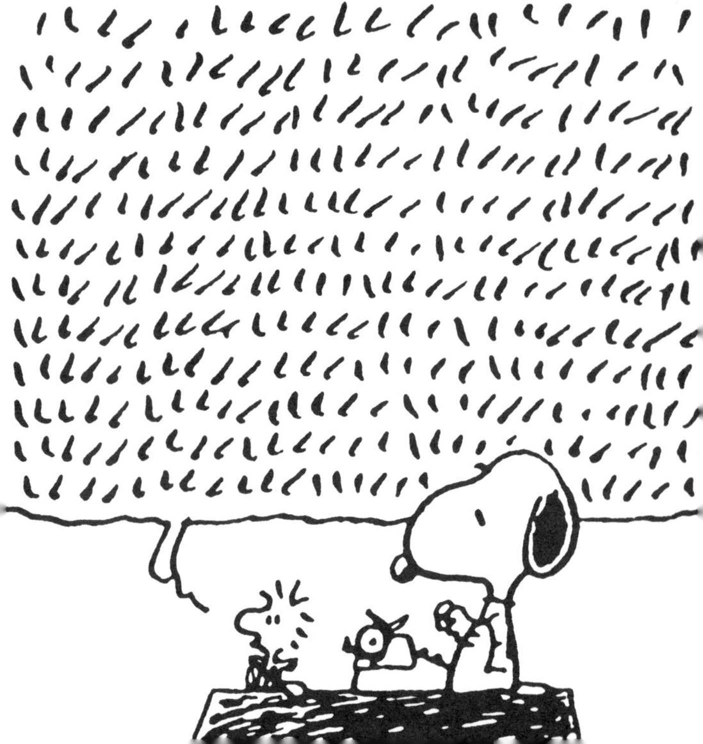

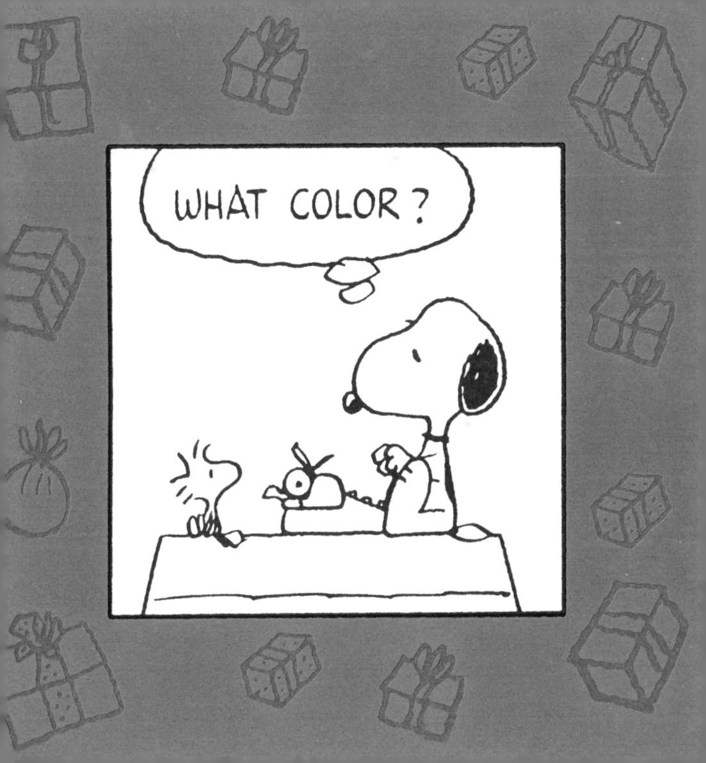
WHAT COLOR?

Dear Santa Claus,
I hope this
letter reaches you
before Christmas.

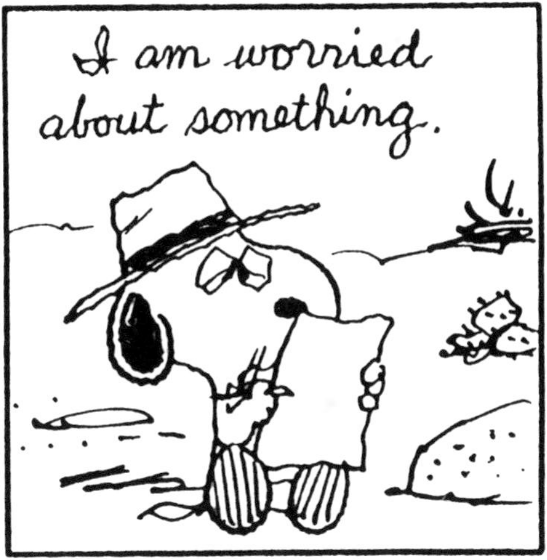
I am worried about something.

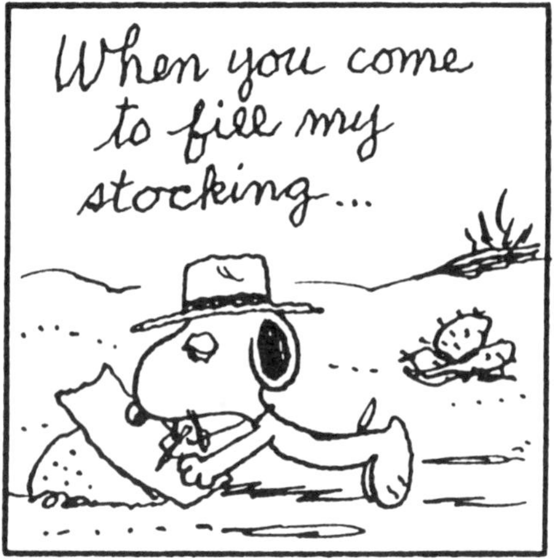
When you come to fill my stocking...

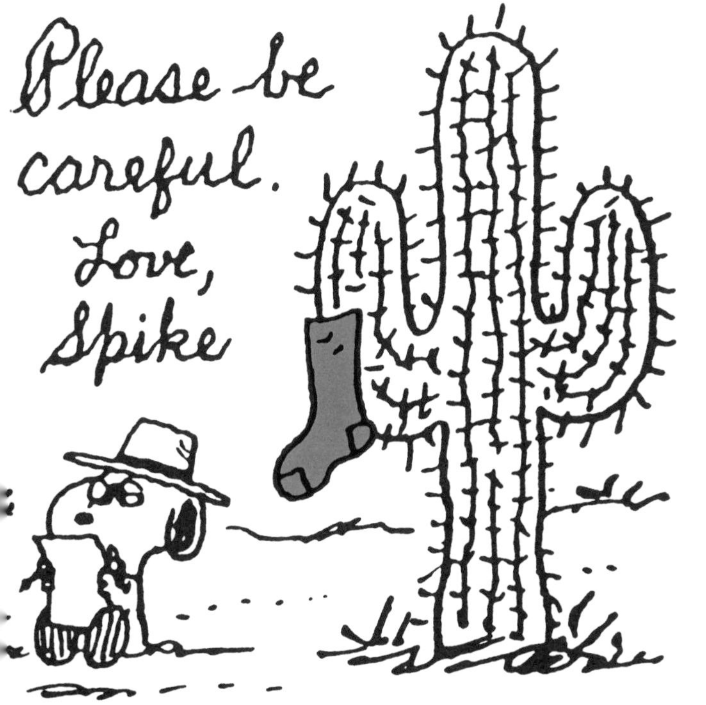
Please be careful. Love, Spike

Christmas
Business

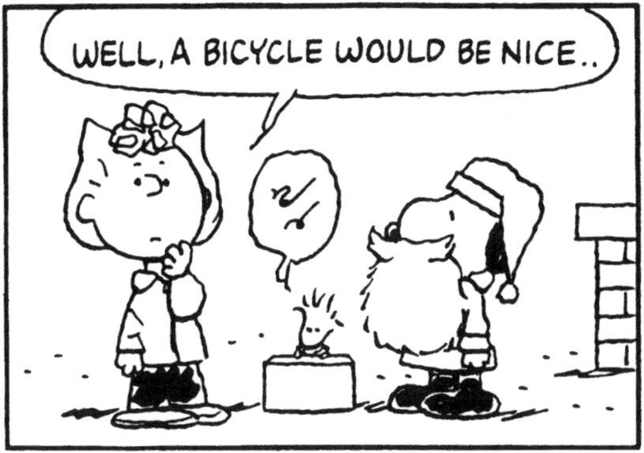
WELL, A BICYCLE WOULD BE NICE..

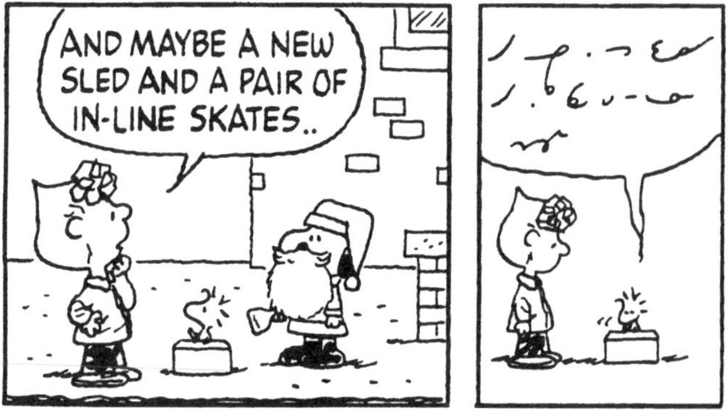
AND MAYBE A NEW SLED AND A PAIR OF IN-LINE SKATES..

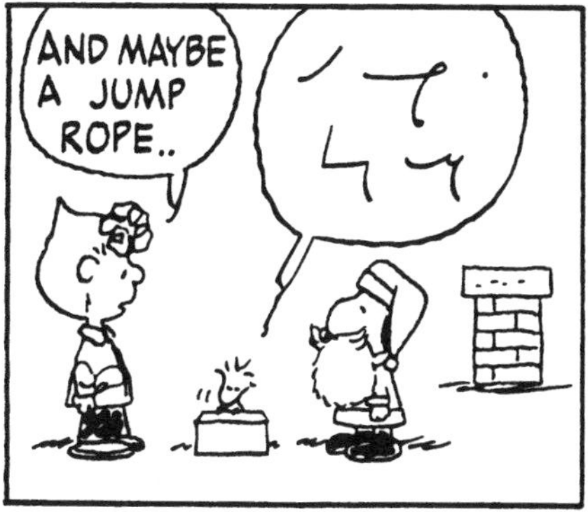
AND MAYBE A JUMP ROPE..

IT'S NICE TO BE ABLE TO TELL SANTA CLAUS WHAT YOU WANT FOR CHRISTMAS, ISN'T IT?
IF YOU CAN GET PAST THE SECRETARY..

Holiday
Lists & Letters

LOOK AT ALL THE PEOPLE I HAVE TO SEND CHRISTMAS CARDS TO!
IF IT BOTHERS YOU, WHY DO YOU DO IT?

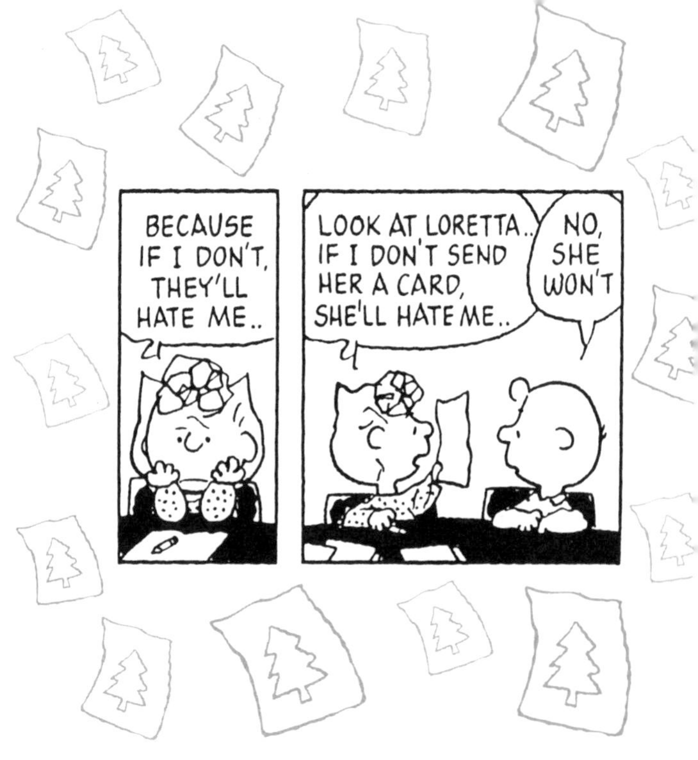
BECAUSE IF I DON'T, THEY'LL HATE ME..
LOOK AT LORETTA.. IF I DON'T SEND HER A CARD, SHE'LL HATE ME..
NO, SHE WON'T

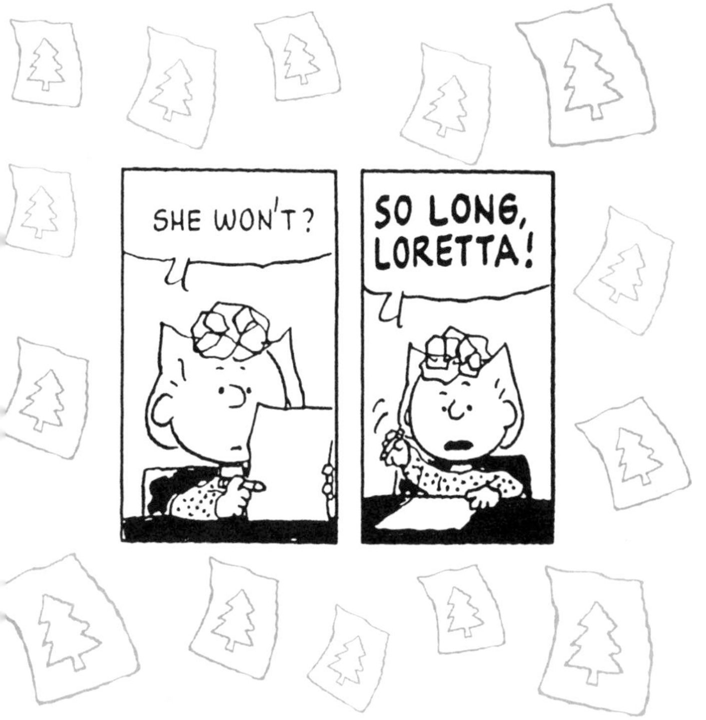
SHE WON'T?
SO LONG, LORETTA!

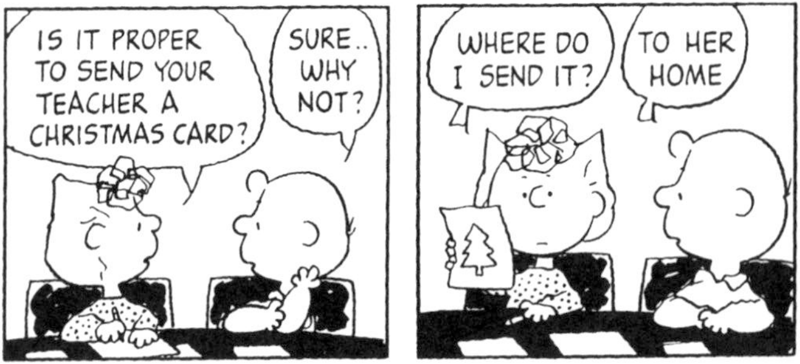
IS IT PROPER TO SEND YOUR TEACHER A CHRISTMAS CARD?
SURE.. WHY NOT?
WHERE DO I SEND IT?
TO HER HOME

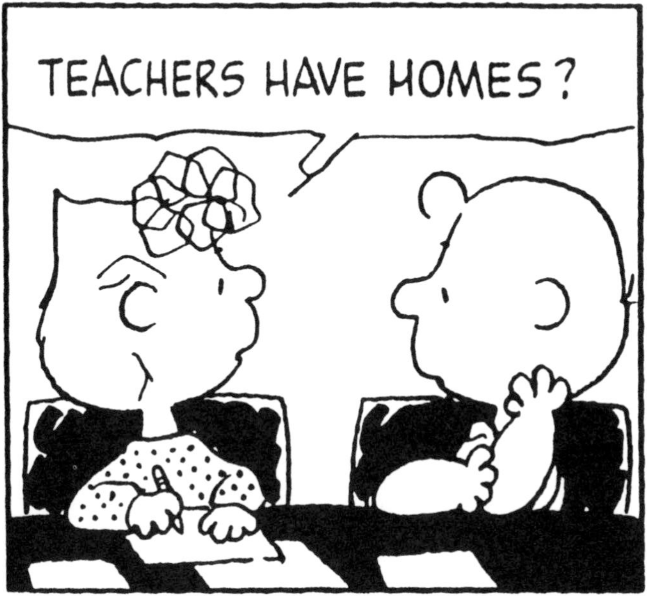
TEACHERS HAVE HOMES?

I'M MAKING OUT
MY CHRISTMAS LIST..
HOW DO YOU SPELL
YOUR NAME?

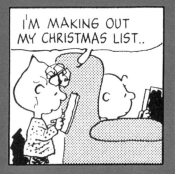

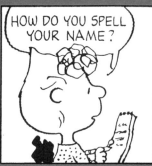

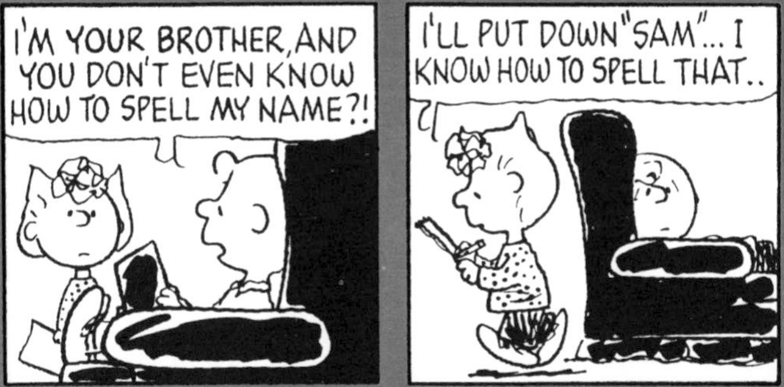
I'M YOUR BROTHER, AND YOU DON'T EVEN KNOW HOW TO SPELL MY NAME?!
I'LL PUT DOWN "SAM"... I KNOW HOW TO SPELL THAT..

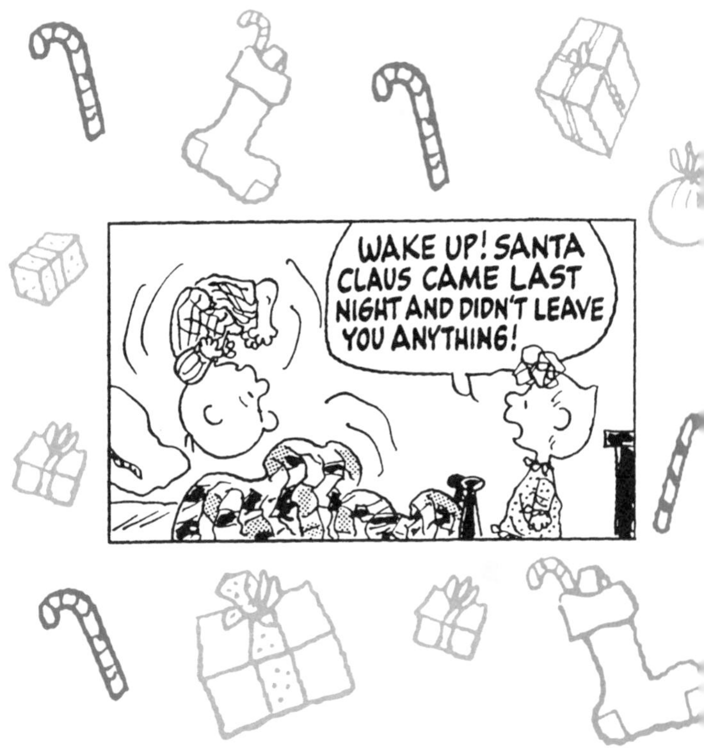
WAKE UP! SANTA CLAUS CAME LAST NIGHT AND DIDN'T LEAVE YOU ANYTHING!

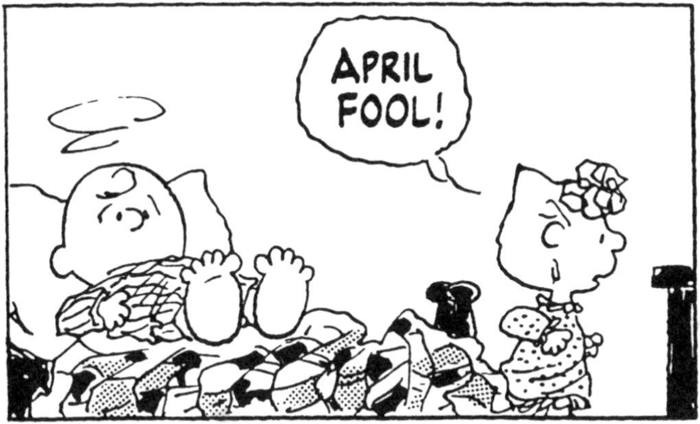
APRIL FOOL!

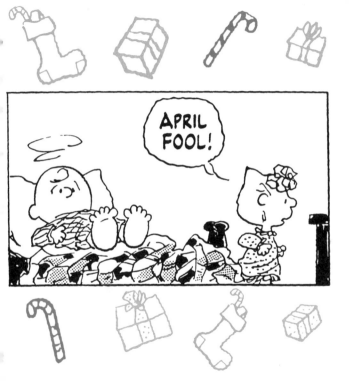

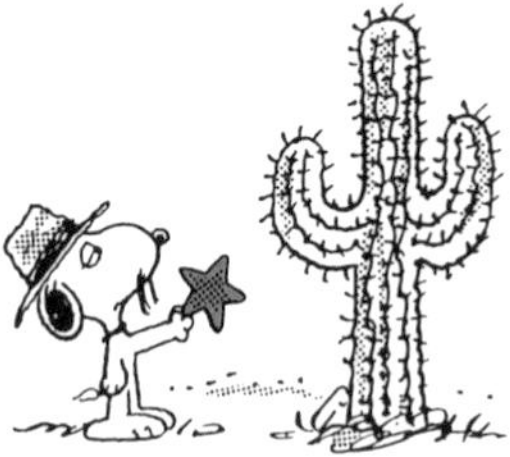

HarperHorizon
An Imprint of HarperCollins*Publishers*

Produced by Jennifer Barry Design, Sausalito, CA
First published in 1998 by HarperCollins*Publishers* Inc.
http://www.harpercollins.com

Lighten Up, It's Christmas! was published by HarperHorizon, an imprint of HarperCollins*Publishers* Inc., 10 East 53rd Street, New York, NY 10022.

Based on the PEANUTS ® comic strip by Charles M. Schulz
http://www.unitedmedia.com

ISBN 0-06-107313-X

Printed in Hong Kong

1 3 5 7 9 10 8 6 4 2

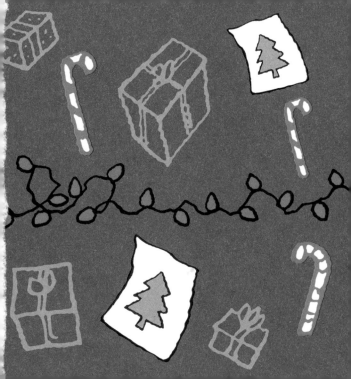

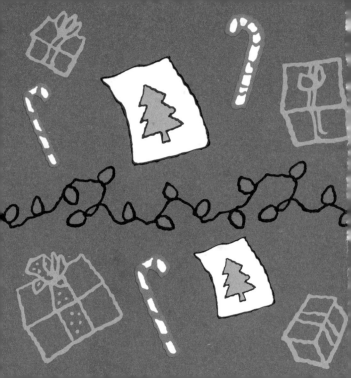